A Note to Parents

Dorling Kindersley Readers is a compelling new program for beginning readers, designed in conjunction with leading literacy experts, including Dr. Linda Gambrell, President of the National Reading Conference and past board member of the International Reading Association.

Beautiful illustrations and superb full-color photographs combine with engaging, easy-to-read stories to offer a fresh approach to each subject in the series. Each *Dorling Kindersley Reader* is guaranteed to capture a child's interest while developing his or her reading skills, general knowledge, and love of reading.

The four levels of *Dorling Kindersley Readers* are aimed at different reading abilities, enabling you to choose the books that are exactly right for your child:

Level 1 – Beginning to read
Level 2 – Beginning to read alone
Level 3 – Reading alone
Level 4 – Proficient readers

The "normal" age at which a child begins to read can be anywhere from three to eight years old, so these levels are intended only as a general guideline.

No matter which level you select, you can be sure that you are helping your child learn to read, then read to learn!

Dorling **DK** Kindersley

LONDON, NEW YORK, SYDNEY, DELHI, PARIS,
MUNICH and JOHANNESBURG

Publisher Neal Porter
Editor Andrea Curley
Art Director Tina Vaughan

U.S. Editor Regina Kahney
Reading Consultant
Linda Gambrell, Ph.D.

Produced by
Shoreline Publishing Group
Art Director Tom Carling,
Carling Design Inc.

Produced in partnership with and licensed by
Major League Baseball Properties, Inc.
Executive Vice President Timothy J. Brosnan
Director of Publishing and MLB Photos
Don Hintze

First American Edition, 2001
Published in the United States by
Dorling Kindersley, Inc.
95 Madison Ave., New York, NY 10016

2 4 6 8 10 9 7 5 3 1
ISBN 0-7894-7349-6 (PLC)   ISBN 0-7894-7348-8 (PB)

Library of Congress Cataloging-in-Publication Data
   Buckley, James, Jr.
   Super Shortstops: Jeter, Nomar, and A-Rod/by James Buckley, Jr. 1st
American ed. p. cm.—(Dorling Kindersley readers)
   ISBN 0-7894-7349-6—ISBN 0-7894-7348-8 (pbk.) 1. Jeter, Derek,
1974- —Juvenile literature. 2. Garciaparra, Nomar, 1973- —Juvenile
literature. 3. Rodriguez, Alex, 1975- —Juvenile literature. 4. Baseball
players—United States—Biography—Juvenile literature. 5. Shortstop
(Baseball) (1. Jeter, Derek, 1974- 2. Garciaparra, Nomar, 1973- 3.
Rodriguez, Alex, 1975- 4. Baseball players.] I. Title. II. Series.

GV865.A1 B84 2001
796.357`092`273—dc21   00-058963

Color reproduction by Colourscan, Singapore.
Printed and bound by L. Rex, China.
Photography credits: t=top, b=below, l=left, r=right, c=center.
All photographs courtesy Major League Baseball Photos except: AP/Wide
World: 9br, 14tl, 15r, 32tl, 33tr, 37br, 39cr; **Balfour:** 21b; **Baseball Hall of
Fame and Library:** 5t, 5b, 6b; **Christies:** 6t; George Curley (Illo.): 4, 16;
Dorling Kindersley: 26tl; **Franklin Sporting Goods:** 30bl; **Georgia Tech:** 34;
Hillerich & Bradsby Co: 38tl ("Silver Slugger" is a service trademark of H&B
Co.); **Miami Boys and Girls Clubs:** 19 David Spindel: 7b, 26bl

see our complete catalog at
www.dk.com

Contents

DORLING KINDERSLEY *READERS*

PROFICIENT
4
READERS

MAJOR LEAGUE BASEBALL™

SUPER SHORTSTOPS
NOMAR, A-ROD, AND JETER

Written by James Buckley, Jr.

A Dorling Kindersley Book

Number 6
Baseball fans use numbers for each position while they keep score of the game. Shortstop is called "6."

A key position

Two outs, ninth inning, home team up by one run. The visitors have a man on third, who is just 90 feet from becoming the tying run.

The batter smashes a ground ball to the right of the shortstop. He dashes over and scoops up the ball. He plants his foot, leaps, twists in the air, and fires a bullet across the diamond to nip the batter by a hair. Game over!

Spectacular plays like that one are made by shortstops every day in baseball. Shortstop is one of baseball's most important defensive positions. Often a team's best fielder plays "short." A shortstop needs quick feet, a great glove, and an accurate throwing arm.

In the hole
The shortstop plays between second and third bases, but closer to second. The area between the shortstop and the third baseman is called "the hole." Shortstops go "into the hole" to make plays.

When baseball was first played in the 1840s, there wasn't a position called shortstop. It wasn't until almost 20 years later that a player began to fill "the hole" between second and third.

One of the greatest players in baseball history was also one of its greatest shortstops. Honus Wagner played from 1897 to 1917. Wagner set a high standard for excellence that shortstops of today are still trying to live up to.

Eeyah!
Hughie "Eeyah" Jennings was another great early shortstop. Playing from 1891 to 1918 he batted over .300 five times.

Wagner was named a member of baseball's All-Century Team in 1999, more than 80 years after he last played.

Cash card
A rare baseball card of Honus Wagner like this one sold at auction in 2000 for more than $1.3 million.

Ouch!
Luke Appling complained of many ailments during his career, but he always managed to play. He played the third most games at shortstop in the 1900s.

Wagner was a great hitter, batting over .300 for 17 seasons in a row. He won eight batting titles, and he retired as baseball's career stolen base leader.

But Wagner was equally great in the field. Legend has it that his hands were so big, he scooped up and threw the ball, dirt, and rocks all at once.

Another story says that a dog once ran on the field and grabbed the ball. Wagner threw the dog and the ball to first base!

Whether those stories are true or not, as a shortstop, Wagner may never be topped.

Another shortstop who could hit well was Luke Appling, who played for the Chicago White Sox from 1930 to 1950. His .388 average in 1936 was the highest by a shortstop in the 1900s.

Viva Luis!
In 1984, Luis Aparicio became the first native of the South American country of Venezuela elected to the Baseball Hall of Fame. Luis played for the White Sox, Orioles, and Red Sox.

Luis Aparicio [app-uh-REE-shee-oh] played for several teams from 1956 to 1973. He played 2,581 games at shortstop, more than any other player. "Little Looie" specialized in speed, leading the league in steals nine times, and defense, winning nine Gold Gloves.

Gold Glove
Top defensive players at each position in each league are awarded this trophy, the Gold Glove.

Up, up in the air! Ozzie Smith was famous for opening each season by taking his position with an awesome running back flip!

While Wagner, Appling, and Aparicio excelled on offense, they were unusual. Most shortstops are depended on for great defense only.

Perhaps the greatest defensive shortstop of all time was Ozzie Smith, who played with San Diego and St. Louis from 1978 to 1996.

Nicknamed "The Wizard of Oz," he could do things with his glove that no one had ever seen. Sliding, diving, leaping, scrambling...he let almost nothing get by him.

While Ozzie became a good hitter by the end of his career, he continued

Cal Ripken, Jr., appeared in 17 consecutive All-Star Games.

the tradition of shortstops who were fielders first, batters last.

And then came a player who changed all that.

Cal Ripken, Jr., was a great defensive shortstop and a top hitter. He was the 1983 Rookie of the Year and a two-time most valuable player (MVP).

He made great defensive plays and then slugged homer after homer. Ripken's all-around success inspired a new generation of shortstops.

Today, three outstanding young shortstops, who are great both at the plate and in the field, are playing—and starring—in the Major Leagues. In this book, read all about A-Rod, Derek, and Nomar!

MVP at short
Barry Larkin of the Reds is another solid shortstop. He was the National League's most valuable player in 1995.

The Streak
Lou Gehrig, "The Iron Horse," held the record for consecutive games played at 2,130. Cal Ripken ended up playing 2,632 games without missing a single one!

9

A-Rod!

Alex Rodriguez stepped to the plate on September 19, 1998. He faced pitcher Jack McDowell of the Angels...and baseball history.

Alex had stolen 40 bases already that season. He also had hit 39 home runs. With one more homer, he would become only the third player—and the first shortstop—to join the "40-40 Club."

The count reached 3-1. Alex stared out at McDowell as the next pitch came in. Alex was only 23, but he was already one of the game's best players.

He swung the bat, and boom! The ball sailed out of the park! The man they called "A-Rod" had done it! There was a new member of the 40-40 club...its youngest yet.

With speed, slugging power, and a powerful arm, A-Rod is one of the best players in baseball.

Mr. Cub
Alex's 42 homers are the second-most ever hit by a shortstop. Two-time MVP Ernie Banks hit 47 home runs in 1958 for the Chicago Cubs.

The first two
Jose Canseco was the first 40-40 player; he did it in 1988. Barry Bonds became the second in 1996.

A-Rod was born in 1975 in New York City. His father, Victor, ran a shoe store. When Alex was a young boy, the family moved back to Victor's homeland, the Dominican Republic.

Alex Rodriguez leads the Seattle Mariners, one of the best young teams in baseball.

Shortstop central
Hundreds of great baseball players have come from the Dominican Republic. The country has produced more than a dozen Major League shortstops.

Top player
USA Baseball, the top amateur organization in the sport, named Alex the best high school player in the country after his senior season.

They later moved to Miami. A sad day came in Alex's life when Victor left the family. Alex's mother, Lourdes [LOR-dess], had to work hard to support her children.

Alex was a superstar from his first time on the diamond. At Westminster Christian High School, he batted .419 and stole 90 bases in 100 games. He was named to the All-America team.

In 1992, his team was named the national champions by *Baseball America*, an important baseball newspaper.

In 1993, Alex was the first player chosen in the Major League baseball draft.

The Seattle Mariners chose wisely. A-Rod played only a season and a half in the minors.

In July, 1995, he became the third 18-year-old pro shortstop since 1900.

Sailors
The Mariners' logo features a compass—a tool for mariners, another name for people who work on the water.

Robin Yount
Like Alex, this Hall of Fame player was also an 18-year-old shortstop. Robin first played in 1974.

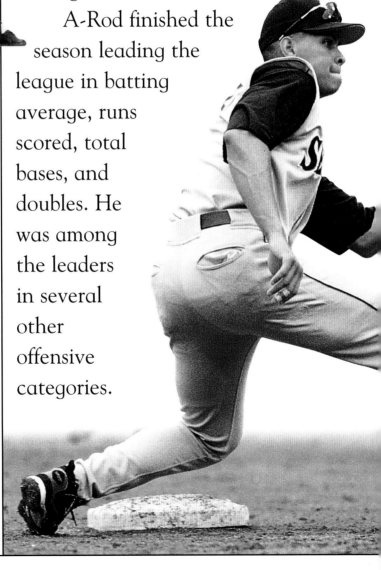

The 1996 season was A-Rod's bust-out year. The kid from Miami proved quickly that he belonged in the big leagues.

Along with playing very well defensively, he smashed records left and right with his bat.

A-Rod finished the season leading the league in batting average, runs scored, total bases, and doubles. He was among the leaders in several other offensive categories.

Joltin' Joe
A-Rod's 1996 average of .358 was the highest by a righthanded hitter since Yankees great Joe DiMaggio hit .381 in 1939.

Stat talk
To find total bases, count singles as one base, doubles as two, triples as three, and home runs as four. A high total means a player had a great season.

In the closest voting in 30 years, A-Rod finished three points behind Texas outfielder Juan Gonzalez for the American League (AL) Most Valuable Player.

A-Rod did win player of the year awards from the Sporting News and the Associated Press.

Longtime fans were amazed at the way young A-Rod combined a powerful bat with speed on the bases and great fielding and throwing ability.

A-Rod was rewriting the rules for how shortstops played. Players like Cal Ripken had paved the way for A-Rod to shine.

Alex demonstrates how a shortstop waits for the throw from the catcher to tag out a baserunner trying to steal second base.

Another good batter
A-Rod's batting title was the first by an AL shortstop since Cleveland's Lou Boudreau in 1944.

Up the middle
Along with fielding ground balls, catching pop flys, and trying to turn double plays, shortstops like Alex must cover second base on tag plays.

Runner

Heads
to second

Fielder
makes tag

Stolen bases
As soon as the pitcher starts to throw to home plate, runners try to move to the next base. If they make it before they are tagged, it's a stolen base.

Baseball fans recognized how special A-Rod was by voting him as the starting shortstop in the 1997 All-Star Game. It was the first time since 1983 that a shortstop other than Cal Ripken, Jr., started the game.

In 1997, A-Rod also began to steal more bases, adding another weapon to his game. He stole 29 bases, setting the stage for his 1998 feats.

A-Rod was not the only great player on the Mariners. Slugging outfielder Ken Griffey, Jr., gave Seattle a one-two punch unmatched in baseball. The team also featured Randy Johnson, one of the hardest-throwing players in baseball history. Together, they led the Mariners to the A.L. Western Division championship. It was the first division title in Seattle history.

The first round of the playoffs are called the "Division Series." Seattle faced the Eastern Division wild-card, the Baltimore Orioles. Although A-Rod batted .313, Seattle lost. He was sad, but he swore to come back better than ever in 1998.

Junior
A-Rod's Seattle teammate, Ken Griffey, Jr., was traded to the Cincinnati Reds after the 1999 season.

All-Star
Each July, Major League Baseball holds the All-Star Game, in which the best players from each league continue a tradition dating to 1933.

Although tall at 6 feet, 3 inches, Alex runs very well and is always a threat to steal.

A hero
"I met Hank Aaron before Opening Day in 1998," Alex says of the all-time home run king. "I really admire him. I have a picture of us together in my locker."

Did he ever! That 1998 season was one of the most remarkable in recent baseball history. Not only did A-Rod slug 42 homers and steal 46 bases, he had 124 runs batted in and a league-leading 213 hits.

His 30th homer made him only the third shortstop with two seasons of 30 or more home runs.

His 36th homer of the season gave him 100 for his short career. He was the fourth-youngest player ever to reach that mark.

A-Rod started the All-Star Game again as one of the game's best players.

Alex helped the Miami Boys and Girls Club buy a new scoreboard for their baseball stadium. He hosts an annual fundraising event for the club, too.

To prove that 1998 wasn't a fluke, his 1999 season was pretty awesome, too, with 42 homers, 111 RBI, and 21 steals. He posted great numbers in 2000 as well.

Alex Rodriguez combines super batting skills, speed on the bases, and great fielding technique like few other shortstops in history!

Look for this superstar on many All-Star teams to come.

The future
"He's young, but that has nothing to do with it," says Alex's Seattle teammate Jay Buhner. "No one works harder, plays harder or gives more than Alex. He'll be a super leader for many years to come."

King of the Yankees

In big games, big-time players get better. That is, really great players do their best when everything is on the line.

With sparkling performances in the 1998 and 1999 World Series, Yankees shortstop Derek Jeter proved that he's one of the biggest players in the game.

While leading New York to two straight four-game Series sweeps, Derek had at least one hit in every game. He batted .353 in the 1999 Series, following his best season ever, when he had 24 home runs and batted .349.

The Yankees have won 25 World Series titles in their history. They have had many great players. And the latest in that long line is a kid from Michigan.

Surrounded by fans and photographers, Derek Jeter celebrates the Yankees' 1999 championship.

The Scooter
Jeter follows in the footsteps of another great New York shortstop, Phil Rizzuto, a member of the Baseball Hall of Fame.

Winning silver
Derek earned this silver ring for helping the Yankees win the 1999 World Series.

Derek was born in Kalamazoo, Michigan. His father, Charles, was a professor and a therapist. His mother, Dorothy, was a teacher.

Education was very important in the Jeter household. But baseball was also important to Derek.

He was a shortstop from the first time he played baseball. And he was a natural at the position.

"I saw an electric player," remembers Yankees scout Dick Groch. "He was thin, but had muscle. He had the perfect infielder's body."

Groch convinced the Yankees that Derek would be a great player someday. Some people with the team thought that Derek would choose college instead, and play pro baseball after he finished school.

"There's only one place this kid's going," Groch said. "Cooperstown."

Cooperstown, New York, is the home of the Baseball Hall of Fame. That's how good they thought young Derek Jeter was.

The Yankees drafted Derek sixth in the 1993 amateur draft.

Derek is not the fastest player in the league, but he is one of the smartest baserunners.

On the lookout
Baseball teams use dozens of scouts to watch high school, college, and Minor League games looking for future stars.

Crystal baseball
"When Derek was in Little League," Derek's father once said, "he said that he was going to play for the Yankees. It's amazing that he grew up to do just that."

Turning two
One of the toughest plays for a shortstop is turning a double play. With a man on first, if a grounder is hit to the second baseman, the shortstop runs to second base. In one motion, he catches the ball, steps on second, then jumps to avoid the sliding baserunner as he throws to first.

Derek joined the Yankees' farm team in the South Atlantic League. The move from high school to the pros was a tough one.

"I cried every night," Jeter said. "I'd never been away from home before. I didn't feel I belonged."

24

Derek struggled through his first pro season. But then, in 1994, he went to Spring Training with the Yankees in Florida.

"I went from playing with my friends in Kalamazoo to playing with guys like Don Mattingly and Wade Boggs," Jeter said.

Along with enjoying playing with the stars, Derek learned a lesson.

"I had the ability to make it," he said. "And I saw how hard I would have to work."

The lessons he learned in Spring Training paid off.

The captain
First baseman Don Mattingly played for the Yankees from 1982-1995. He was a big help to Derek as the youngster adjusted to life in the pros.

Short visit
Like Derek did with the Yankees in 1995, players who spend only a few games with a Major League team are said to have had "a cup of coffee" in the Majors.

Top rookie
Baseball's rookie of the year receives the Jackie Robinson Award, named for the first African-American to play in the Majors, in 1947.

JACKIE ROBINSON
outfield BROOKLYN DODGERS

Derek played in only 15 games for the Yankees in 1995, but several of them came during the pennant race in September. He remembers thinking at the time, "Man, this is where I've got to be."

In 1996, he was there to stay. He was the team's first Opening Day rookie shortstop since 1962. And in his first game with New York, Derek slugged a home run!

That was the beginning of a great season for Derek and the Yankees. He was named the Rookie of the Year...and the Yankees won their first World Series since 1981.

Derek continued to improve in 1997, and blossomed into a superstar in 1998, with 19 homers, 84 RBI, and a .324 batting average. He finished third in the voting for Most Valuable Player. But more importantly, he helped the Yankees win another World Championship.

Leader of the Yanks
"Derek has become the leader of this team at only 24 years old," Yankees pitcher David Cone said. "He leads by example with his bat, his glove, and his legs."

Number 5
The number five on Derek's sleeve was worn by the Yankees in 2000 to honor Joe DiMaggio, who died in late 1999. Derek wears number 2.

First game
Opening Day in baseball is a very important day. Most teams decorate the stadium and introduce the entire team.

Derek's work in the field continued to amaze fans and other players. His hitting improved every season. As the Yankees' shortstop, he had a lot of responsibility, too.

27

Golden award
Winning teams in the World Series get this trophy. The Yankees have earned 25 World Series championship trophies.

New jersey?
No, Derek's not sporting a new Yankees' jersey style. Many players wear lightweight jackets or shirts like this one during pregame warmups.

Derek continued to be a leader in 1999. In September, he hit two home runs in a game against Boston and helped New York clinch another A.L. Eastern Division title.

He set career highs with 24 home runs, 102 runs batted in (RBI), and a .349 batting average.

In the World Series, Derek led the Yankees to another four-game sweep. He extended his World Series hitting streak to 12 games.

Derek, like Alex Rodriguez, has helped make shortstop an important all-around position. The Yankees depend on Derek for his bat, his glove, and his leadership. Today's young shortstops are changing the way the position is played.

That's all Derek would change.

"I wouldn't change anything else," he said. "I have the greatest job in the world. Only one person can have it. You have shortstops on other teams—and I'm not knocking other teams—but there's only one shortstop on the Yankees."

Manager's words
"Derek is everything we've hoped he'd be and more," Yankees manager Joe Torre says. "The sky's the limit for him."

Giving back
In 1996, Derek started the Turn 2 Foundation to raise money to help kids stay away from drugs and alcohol.

The Olde Towne Team

The Red Sox have been playing in Boston since 1901. They were once known as the Pilgrims.

Batting glove
Hitters wear these leather and nylon gloves to get a better grip on the bat.

Pride of Boston

Watching Nomar Garciaparra [garr-see-uh-PAR-uh] get ready to bat is like watching a spider dance. Everything is moving at once.

First, the Red Sox star shortstop puts his bat down between his feet. Then he tugs on the bottom of each batting glove six or seven times, very quickly.

Then he grabs the bat again and steps into the batter's box.

But he's not ready yet. Then he taps each toe several times on the ground, one after the other, tap, tap, tap, tap, and wiggles his bat.

Finally, he's ready to hit.

Nomar may have some strange habits at the plate, but all that tugging and tapping must work. He has become one of baseball's best all-around players.

Nomar Garciaparra takes a long time getting ready to hit...but when he's finally ready, watch out!

Nomar was born in Whittier, California. He played several sports, but he was most serious about baseball. When he was young, his baseball teammates called him "No-Nonsense Nomar."

Feet first
Nomar, like most kickers, booted a football just like a soccer player shoots a soccer ball.

Why Nomar?
Can you figure out where Nomar's unusual name comes from? Here's a hint: His father's name is Ramon. If you still can't guess, just spell Ramon backward!

Nomar had superstitions even back then. He never let anyone touch his glove, and he never threw or kicked it.

One thing he did kick was a soccer ball. He played for his high school team. He also was a field-goal kicker for the football team.

But back on the diamond was where he shined. Nomar's high school team in Whittier won the league championship in 1990 and 1991.

One of Nomar's early coaches was his father, Ramon.

"My dad made me play every position so I would learn them and have respect for the kids playing them," Nomar said.

"At dinner, we would outline plays on napkins and he would quiz me on game situations," Nomar added. "At his office, I'd sometimes play ball in the hallway. My dad taught me all about the game."

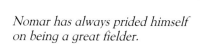

Nomar has always prided himself on being a great fielder.

Star power
After he became a star with the Red Sox, soccer fan Nomar got a chance to kick around the soccer ball with Women's World Cup star Mia Hamm.

Buzz
Georgia Tech
sports teams
are known as
the Yellow
Jackets; that's a
type of wasp.

Feel a draft?
Each June,
Major League
teams select, or
"draft," players
from high
schools and
colleges to join
their teams.

Nomar was drafted by the
Milwaukee Brewers after high
school. But he decided to go to
college. His talents helped him earn
a scholarship to
attend Georgia
Tech University in
Atlanta,
Georgia.

*Nomar played three
seasons at Georgia Tech.
The school's full name is
the Georgia Institute of
Technology.*

At Georgia Tech, he teamed with a big catcher named Jason Varitek, who would one day be his teammate on the Red Sox.

Nomar and Jason led Georgia Tech to the College World Series, held each June in Omaha, Nebraska.

Along with being a great glove man in the field, Nomar was becoming an offensive powerhouse.

In three seasons at Georgia Tech, he batted .372 and had 58 doubles, 23 home runs, and 166 RBI.

In 1992, Nomar got the chance to represent his country by playing in the Summer Olympics. Baseball had been a demonstration sport before, but in 1992, it became a full medal sport.

At the Games in Barcelona, Spain, the United States team, led by many future pros, reached the semifinals.

Rings of gold
The five rings in the Olympic symbol stand for five continents: Asia, Europe, North America, South America, and Africa.

El béisbol
[el bays-BOL] means baseball in Spanish. Cuba won gold medals in 1992 and 1996.

Oops

Just like hitters and pitchers, players on defense, such as Nomar at shortstop, have statistics. For instance, when a fielder makes a mistake such as dropping a ball or throwing the ball past his teammate, he is charged with an "error."

A is for effort

Baseball's minor league teams play in four groups, each more advanced than the last: Rookie, A, AA, and AAA. "Triple A" is one stop before the Majors.

Nomar says he is "blessed with quick feet and quick hands." That comes in handy on close plays at second base.

In 1994, the Boston Red Sox selected Nomar with the 12th pick of the draft. This time, he decided that it was time to head to the pros.

Nomar spent the 1994 season in the minor leagues. First, he played in Florida and Arizona.

In 1995, he moved up to play with the Trenton Thunder in Double-A. He set a team record with 35 stolen bases, and led league shortstops in number of plays made.

In 1996, Nomar played in Triple-A for the Pawtucket Red Sox in Rhode Island. He was chosen the player of the year by his teammates, while setting a team record for shortstops with 16 home runs.

All through his time in the Minor Leagues Nomar was perfecting his skills. He made himself a better hitter. He took hundreds of ground balls. He practiced over and over. You would think that a player who was already as good as Nomar wouldn't have to work so hard.

But working hard is how Nomar succeeded. No matter how successful he was, he never stopped trying to get better. In 1997, all his hard work began to pay off.

The Minors
Some Minor League teams, like the PawSox, take the name of their Major League "parent."

Way before Nomar
Hall of Fame shortstop Joe Cronin starred for the Boston Red Sox from 1935-1945.

Silver bat
The top batter at each position receives the Silver Slugger™ award.

Batter up
The "leadoff" hitter bats first in the lineup. Usually, he is good at getting on base and doesn't hit many homers. Nomar showed that a leadoff hitter could do both.

Nomar's first full season in the Majors was 1997, but it was one of the best ever for a shortstop.

Among Nomar's 1997 stats:

• He led the majors with 684 at-bats, setting a team record.

• He led all AL rookies in 13 offensive categories.

• He set a Red Sox rookie record with 209 hits.

• He set a rookie record by hitting in 30 straight games.

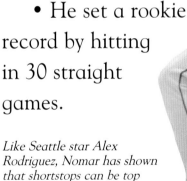

Like Seattle star Alex Rodriguez, Nomar has shown that shortstops can be top sluggers, too.

Not surprisingly, Nomar was named to the AL All-Star team; he was the first Red Sox rookie all-star since 1975.

Batting leadoff and playing outstanding defense, Nomar helped make the Red Sox into a much better ballclub. Few players in

baseball history have had such an outstanding rookie season. Not surprisingly, Nomar was named Rookie of the Year.

Believe it or not, he did even better in 1998, batting .323, with 35 homers and 122 RBI.

Mr. Yawkey
Nomar also won the Thomas Yawkey Award for being the Red Sox most valuable player. Yawkey (center) owned the team from 1933-1976.

RBI, not RBIs
The important statistic called "runs batted in" is abbreviated RBI, not RBIs, because they are not called "Runs batted ins"!

Pedro the great
Star pitcher Pedro Martinez came up big for the Red Sox in the 1999 playoffs after winning the Cy Young award for the season.

Shortstop pals
Two great shortstops, New York's Derek Jeter and Boston's Nomar Garciaparra, met on the field during the 1999 All-Star Game.

The Red Sox lost to the Cleveland Indians in the 1998 Divisional Playoffs, but Nomar did set a series record 11 RBI and batted .333.

In 1999, Nomar won the AL batting championship with a .357 average. Again, the Red Sox earned a Wild-Card playoff spot. And again, they played the Indians.

This time, the Red Sox had another ace: pitcher Pedro Martinez.

After losing the first two games to Cleveland, the Red Sox put on an amazing rally. In Game Five, Boston trailed the Indians, first 5-2, and later 8-7. Martinez shut down Cleveland with six perfect innings.

Meanwhile, Nomar had a home run and three RBI, and Troy O'Leary hit a grand slam. The Red Sox won 12-8 in one of the most memorable playoff games in years.

The Red Sox lost in the next round, but with a talented player like Nomar on their side, Boston can have playoff dreams every year.

Move ahead
After the 1999 playoff loss to the Yankees, Nomar said, "Are we disappointed? Sure, I'm sorry any season we don't win the World Series. But I'm not going to hang my head. We'll be back."

Who's next?

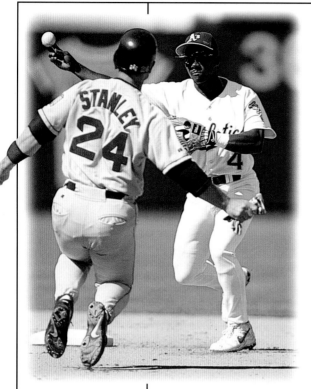

Alex Rodriguez, Derek Jeter, and Nomar Garciaparra followed in a long line of great Major League shortstops. So who is going to follow these three great players?

There are a number of great young shortstops

Tejada fires to first to complete a double play.

playing right now, waiting to make their mark.

In Oakland, Miguel Tejada [tay-HA-dah] combines great fielding talent with a powerful bat. Miguel is the latest in a long line of great shortstops from the Dominican Republic.

Miguel, who is only 25, had more than 20 home runs in each of his first two full seasons, and

On the move
Tejada's team, the Oakland Athletics, formerly played in Philadelphia and Kansas City before moving to Oakland in 1968.

helped the Athletics become one of baseball's top young teams.

In New York, Mets' shortstop Rey Ordonez [RAY or-DOHN-yez] has been compared to the great Ozzie Smith. Rey, who is from Cuba, makes awesome sliding catches and springs quickly to his feet to throw runners out. He had an incredible .994 fielding average in 1999.

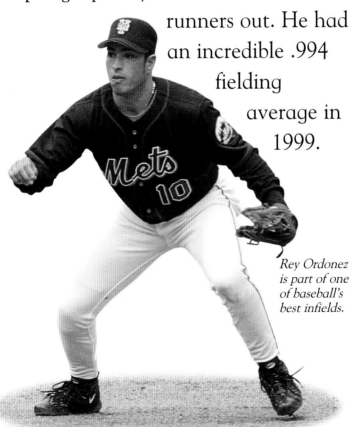

Rey Ordonez is part of one of baseball's best infields.

Rey's home
Rey is one of several top players who have come from Cuba in recent years. The Caribbean island nation has a long tradition of great baseball.

Fielding average
To figure out a player's fielding average, divide his number of chances without errors by the number of chances; that is, how many times he caught or threw the ball.

Speed demon
Tony Womack spent the first five seasons of his career with the Pittsburgh Pirates before joining Arizona in 1999. Tony also uses his speed to play outfield once in a while.

In Arizona, Diamondbacks shortstop Tony Womack brings another powerful weapon to the game: speed. Tony is among the National League's top basestealing threats. In 1999, he led the league with 72 stolen bases. He also stole 60 bases in 1998.

Another top young shortstop is Edgar Renteria of St. Louis. A native of the South American country of Colombia, he earned his first All-Star game berth in 2000.

Although he is only 26 years old, Edgar has played five Major League seasons. He began his career in 1996 with the Florida Marlins. In his second season, he helped them win the World Series! Edgar joined the Cardinals in 1999 and the change of scenery has helped him.

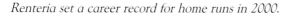

Renteria set a career record for home runs in 2000.

A solid fielder, he has become a much better hitter.

Shortstops are becoming more than just great glove men. They're becoming key parts of their teams' offense. Look for more from A-Rod, Derek, Nomar, and the rest in the years to come.

ALEX RODRIGUEZ
Born: 7/27/75
Weight: 190
Height: 6′ 3″
Bats: Right
Throws: Right

Three amigos

In baseball, numbers often tell the story. On these pages you'll find the complete Major League records for the three super shortstops featured in this book. You can follow their progress in the seasons ahead and record their final stats in the spaces provided. Sharpen those pencils and start counting the homers, RBI, and steals of these three great players.

ALEX RODRIGUEZ

Year	HR	RBI	Avg.	Steals
1994	0	2	.204	3
1995	5	19	.232	4
1996	36	123	.358	15
1997	23	84	.300	29
1998	42	124	.310	46
1999	42	111	.285	21
2000	___	___	___	___
2001	___	___	___	___
2002	___	___	___	___

DEREK JETER

Year	HR	RBI	Avg.	Steals
1995	0	7	.250	0
1996	10	78	.314	14
1997	10	70	.291	23
1998	19	84	.324	30
1999	24	102	.349	19
2000	—	—	—	—
2001	—	—	—	—
2002	—	—	—	—

DEREK JETER
Born: 6/26/74
Weight: 175
Height: 6′ 3″
Bats: Right
Throws: Right

NOMAR GARCIAPARRA

Year	HR	RBI	Avg.	Steals
1996	4	16	.241	0
1997	30	98	.306	9
1998	35	122	.323	6
1999	27	104	.357	3
2000	—	—	—	—
2001	—	—	—	—
2002	—	—	—	—

NOMAR GARCIAPARRA
Born: 7/23/73
Weight: 165
Height: 6′
Bats: Right
Throws: Right

Glossary

Assist
On defense, a player gets an assist when he makes a throw that leads to an out.

Count
The number of balls and strikes on a hitter. For instance, "the count is three and one" means three balls and one strike.

Diamond
The playing field for baseball. The infield actually forms a square, but tipped on one end to form a diamond shape.

Error
A mistake made by a fielder that allows a batter to reach base or a baserunner to advance safely. Plays are called hits or errors by an official scorer who sits in the press box.

Expansion team
A team newly added to the Major Leagues.

Fielding average
Measures a player's success at throwing and catching. Figure fielding average by dividing total chances by errors.

40-40 Club
A special group of players who have hit 40 or more homers and stolen 40 or more bases in one season.

Glove man
Slang term for a great fielder.

Hall of Fame
Located in Cooperstown, New York, this building houses baseball memorabilia and honors the greatest players of the past.

Minor Leagues
Lower levels of professional baseball. Players advance through the minors to the Major Leagues.

Opening Day
The special name given to the first day of the season.

Putout
Awarded to the defensive player who tags out an offensive player or touches a base to record an out.

Shortstop
Baseball defensive position that plays between second and third bases.

Spring training
Held in February and March in Florida and Arizona; teams use this time to prepare for the upcoming season.

Stolen base
When on base, a player can advance to another base as the pitcher throws home. If he makes it, he has "stolen" the base.

Streak
In sports, a streak is any series of games or moments that add up to a great feat. For instance, a "hitting streak" means getting at least one hit in any number of games in a row.